SAINT ROSE PHILIPPINE
DUCHESNE

A Heart on Fire
across Frontiers

Carolyn Osiek, RSCJ

SAINT ROSE PHILIPPINE DUCHESNE
A Heart on Fire across Frontiers

Cover Illustration by Emil Frei studios
Book design by Peggy Nehmen, n-kcreative.com

Printed in the United States of America
ISBN-13: 978-0-9971329-1-5

Published by

 Society of the Sacred Heart™
United States – Canada

4120 Forest Park Avenue
St. Louis Missouri 63108-2809
314-652-1500
www.rscj.org

 @RSCJUSC
facebook.com/SocietyoftheSacredHeart
facebook.com/ReligiousOfTheSacredHeart
(Vocations)

CONTENTS

INTRODUCTION

OVER THE YEARS, there have been numerous short studies of Rose Philippine Duchesne. More recently better access to the originals of her writings has enabled deeper insights into her ways of seeing her world. Philippine was very much part of the mindset of the *ancient régime* of Europe in which she had grown up, and she carried with her all her life many of the assumptions of that world. Yet she looked always to the horizon, to what lay beyond, to the *more* that could be done for God.

As we celebrate the bicentennial of Philippine's arrival in the New World with her four companions, we too look to the horizon of God's future. May she be a familiar companion along the way.

I am grateful to Pamela Schaeffer and Donna Heckler for their helpful editing suggestions and to Kathleen Hughes, RSCJ, and the Bicentennial Committee for providing the context and the excitement about celebrating two hundred years of mission.

—Carolyn Osiek, RSCJ

HAPPY BEGINNINGS

ROSE PHILIPPINE DUCHESNE, the courageous pioneer who would take her beloved Society of the Sacred Heart to new, international frontiers, was born in Grenoble, France, on August 29, 1769. She was the second of eight children of Pierre-François Duchesne, member of the Parliament of Grenoble, and Rose-Euphrosine Perier. The house where she grew up was in a prominent location on the main square of the city and next door to the home of her mother's brother, Claude Perier, his wife, Marie-Charlotte Pascal, and their twelve children. Although these were mostly happy times for the children of this large, extended family, Philippine's childhood was marked by two unfortunate events. When she was three years old, she contracted smallpox, which scarred her face for life. Then, some six years later, her older sister, Marie-Adelaide died, making the nine-year-old Philippine the oldest of the Duchesne siblings and second oldest of the combined households.

Most of the children in these two families of the *haute bourgeoisie* were privately tutored. As was the custom, Philippine and her cousin Josephine Perier, just one year younger and her lifelong best friend, were sent together in 1781 to boarding school at the Visitation convent of Sainte Marie d'En-Haut in order to prepare for their First Communion. Soon after this event, in May 1782, Philippine's father learned of her interest in entering the convent and abruptly withdrew her from the school. But she would return a few years later, for Sainte Marie, perched on a hillside high above the city, was the place where her missionary longings began. The confessor of the students had been a missionary among the Native Americans of Illinois, in North America, and his stories stirred up in Philippine thoughts of becoming a missionary herself. By the time of her First Communion at the age of twelve, it was her dream to become a religious and to announce the Gospel in foreign lands.

Philippine returned to her family and continued private studies in foreign languages and, despite little native talent, pursued interests in drawing, music, and dance. One of her sisters remarked that Philippine worked as hard at learning dance as she did at learning algebra. At the age of seventeen, this firm resolve set her on a life course that would lead her to refuse a marriage proposal and declare her intention to enter religious life as a Visitation nun at Sainte Marie. When her parents denied permission, she turned to another family member. One day in the spring of 1788, in Philippine's eighteenth year, she asked one of her aunts to accompany her to Sainte Marie to visit the nuns. Once there, Philippine declared that she was entering the community and refused to leave. In spite of the dismay and efforts of her family to bring her home, she remained.

Photo L. Lieux, RSCJ

Stairs to the monastery of Sainte Marie d'En-Haut

Courtyard of Sainte Marie d'En-Haut

INTO—AND OUT OF—RELIGIOUS LIFE

PHILIPPINE WAS HAPPY at Sainte Marie, and had the political situation not exploded around her, she would have remained a Religious of the Visitation for the rest of her life, as did four of her aunts on her father's side and, later, one of her sisters, who had entered a Visitation convent at Romans. But fate was to have it otherwise. The Parliament of Grenoble was deeply involved in the growing opposition to suppression of political rights by the monarchy. Around the time that Philippine entered the convent at Sainte Marie, the Grenoble parliament rejected the central government's attempt to sharply reduce parliament's power. The revolt spread throughout the country.

In an attempt to resolve the crisis, the first meeting of the Estates-General of Dauphiny took place at Vizille, the Perier chateau near Grenoble, on July 21, 1788. Philippine's father missed the second meeting, which took place at Romans on September 9 of that year, to attend Philippine's clothing in the Visitation habit the following day. A year later, he withdrew temporarily from politics but foreseeing what lay ahead, refused permission for Philippine to make her vows. Indeed, by October 1789, all religious vows were suspended in France, and by September 1792, the Visitation community was forced to disband. Philippine accompanied her family to their chateau at nearby Grâne. Thus began eleven years of uncertainty in the young woman's life, as she was forced to put her desire for religious life on hold. What then was she to do with her life?

During the worst part of the Reign of Terror (September 1793–July 1794), the old monastery of Sainte Marie became a prison for priests and religious who refused to cooperate with the anti-clerical revolutionaries now in control. Philippine and her cousin Josephine spent part of their time in Grenoble, working with an association of women who risked their lives to visit priests who were imprisoned or in hiding, and to assist their efforts to clandestinely take the Eucharist to the homes of the sick and dying. Philippine herself never wrote of this, but later, her sister Euphrosine told how the two of them would go into the most frightful places to minister to those in need, especially imprisoned priests and religious.

When the Terror was over, Philippine discovered images of Saint Francis Regis and Saint Francis Xavier in the parish church of Grâne. Her devotion to the two Jesuit missionary saints grew. In 1800 she made a pilgrimage to the nearby shrine of Saint Francis Regis at La Louvesc. That experience proved decisive, and she returned to Grenoble, eager to perform some charitable work. She found that instruction of girls was well underway, but poor boys were being neglected. So she gathered a group of street boys, enticing them first with food, then religious instruction. They became devoted to her, and sometimes greeted her in the street, causing great embarrassment to her family and friends.

Meanwhile, Philippine had taken on the dream of acquiring the old monastery of Sainte Marie from the government and making it possible for the Visitation community to reassemble there. Family members influential in local politics, especially Philippine's uncle Claude Perier, obtained from the government the right to lease the monastery. To Philippine's chagrin, the lease was in her name alone rather than that of the former superior, Mother Anne-Félicité de Murinais. Under pressure from her uncle, Philippine signed the document anyway. On December 10, 1801, for 800 francs annual rent, the monastery of Sainte-Marie d'En Haut was hers.

The house was in a terrible state of disrepair, and returning it to a habitable condition became Philippine's total responsibility and cost. When people learned that a novice of the former convent, rather than the superior, was trying to gather the dispersed community, rumors flew. Although in reality, Philippine wanted Mother de Murinais to come and take up her position of leadership, others wondered. Did Philippine want to be the new superior? Who did she think she was? When Mother de Murinais did eventually return, along with several other aging community members, it had been ten years since the dispersal. Mother de Murinais was more than eighty years old, and restoring the community as it had been simply would not work.

In letting go of her dream to reconstitute the Visitation community, which Philippine had believed to be the will of God, she faced a profound spiritual crisis. She was left with two or three former nuns and six or eight boarding students entrusted to them by local families for their education. Local gossip had it that Philippine had been too difficult to deal with. It is possible that her efforts were hindered by her strong and definite ideas about how religious life should be lived.

She did, however, receive support from several influential priests. One drew up a rule for the community under the name of "Daughters of the Propagation of the Faith," and Philippine pronounced simple vows at her beloved Sainte Marie on March 3, 1803. The boarding school continued to attract students, which enabled it to be self-supporting. But what was to follow? Through one of the priests, Philippine heard about Father Joseph Varin, advisor and spiritual guide of the leader of a newly-founded women's congregation dedicated to the Sacred Heart (though at the time they could not use that name). This impressive young woman, Madeleine Sophie Barat, who came from a town in Burgundy, was well educated and, though just twenty-five years old, possessed evident gifts of spiritual leadership.

Meeting of Sophie Barat and Philippine Duchesne

3

THE ENCOUNTER OF TWO SAINTS

FATHER VARIN VISITED Philippine's monastery at the end of July 1804 to celebrate the feast of Saint Ignatius with the nuns. Philippine's eagerness to pursue this new direction led her to a show of impatience when he appeared to be leaving without saying anything definite. Father Varin countered that God works slowly. "On the contrary," she interjected, alluding to Psalm 19:6. "Scripture says that he leaps with great bounds." He laughed and agreed that he must send Mother Barat as soon as possible to found a convent of the new congregation at Sainte Marie.

"As soon as possible" turned into five months of eager waiting by a not very patient Philippine. She did not know that a few months after his visit, Father Varin had written to Sophie, telling her that Philippine was a great and generous soul for whom she should make the journey to Grenoble. Finally, on December 13, 1804, Sophie arrived in Grenoble with two companions from her first foundation in Amiens.

The day before, December 12, had been Sophie's twenty-fifth birthday. Philippine was ten years older and from a significantly more distinguished family. Nevertheless, Philippine immediately acknowledged Sophie as superior and guide. Many years later, Sophie told the story of her arrival at the door of Sainte Marie. At the threshold of the convent, there was a flurry of movement, and suddenly Philippine was at her feet murmuring something about "how beautiful on the mountains are the feet of those who bring peace," an allusion to Isaiah 52:7. "I was so astonished, I let her do it," Sophie remembered, indirectly underscoring a quality of impetuousness that characterized Philippine in these years of young adulthood.

The little group, now under the personal direction of Sophie, the young superior, and Father Varin, began to live religious life in earnest. In January, the new novices made a ten-day retreat, while the sisters who had come with Sophie continued to maintain the boarding school. The following year, on November 21, 1805, Philippine and six companions pronounced their vows in the Society of the Sacred Heart; it was the fifth anniversary of the first consecration of Sophie and her original companions in Paris.

Philippine's missionary vocation was not far behind. While happily engaged in the life of the community and the boarding school at Grenoble, she began to realize that she was called beyond the world she knew. On the morning of January 10, 1806, less than two months after pronouncing her vows, she was reflecting in her morning meditation on the recent feast of Epiphany, particularly on how the Magi had set out for a foreign land, leaving their own land behind. She realized that if she were to follow the missionary call, she would have to leave behind her beloved Sainte Marie, in which she had invested both considerable labor and even part of her inheritance. Nevertheless, she then and there made the decision to sacrifice the monastery and all that was meant by home.

Philippine's generous, spontaneous and somewhat impulsive character is once again revealed in this decision. Although her missionary desires were not yet well thought out, she loved to pray before the Blessed Sacrament during the hours of the night and even asked to spend the entire night in prayer. Sophie did not often give permission, reminding her that normally she needed at least five hours of sleep in order to carry on the demanding work of community and school. However, on the next Holy Thursday, April 3, 1806, Sophie did give permission for an all-night vigil. The next day, Philippine recounted the content of that vigil prayer in a letter to Sophie, reporting that she had spent the night in the company of Saints Francis Regis and Xavier, bringing Christ to the New World.

Four months later, Sophie's answer from the port of Bordeaux was from her heart, giving hope that the dream might soon come to fulfillment: "I stood on the wharf watching…a number of ships from all over the world that had come into port…," Sophie wrote in a letter dated August 30, 1806. "It seemed to me that we were both here in this city, ready to embark on one of these vessels, to go at last where your desires are calling you."

Yet, it would be another twelve years before that happy day arrived.

In October 1815, Philippine was called from the house of Grenoble to the General Council of the Society in Paris. The Council was a pivotal event in which the line of authority in the Society was clarified and the Constitutions were formally adopted for the first time. Philippine's careful minutes of the event provide crucial information about the history of the Society at this period. At the end of the meeting, she was elected secretary general, requiring her to take up residence in Paris. As far as we know, she never returned to Grenoble. She was now at the center of the Society's activity, meeting everyone who came and went at the motherhouse. As she had kept the house journal in Grenoble during her residence there, so she did in Paris as well. In it, she noted for October 21, 1816, that "a letter from Father Barat [Sophie's brother] gives hope, after a conversation he had with Bishop [Louis William] Dubourg of New Orleans, that our Society will be able to be established in his diocese."

Her excitement must have been overwhelming as she wrote those words. Bishop Dubourg, newly appointed as bishop of the entire territory of the Louisiana Purchase, was in Europe for several years recruiting priests, seminarians, and sisters for his vast new diocese. Hope continued to grow, in spite of Mother Barat's apparent reluctance to authorize such a project. Then on May 16, 1817, Bishop Dubourg came for a final visit to the motherhouse in Paris. As Sophie was about to send him away empty-handed, Philippine knelt before her and beseeched her to give consent for an establishment in the New World. This dramatic gesture must have been convincing. Philippine wrote in the house journal for that day that Mother Barat "has promised him six religious for next spring."

4

ON TO AMERICA

THE 1818 DEPARTURE had been planned for after Easter, but it was advanced to February because of plans for an earlier departure by Father Bernard Martial, Bishop Dubourg's vicar-general, and several other priests able to be traveling companions for the religious. The preceding months were marked by a flurry of preparations, including the gathering of objects that would be useful in America, and the choice of the missionary sisters who would go. Philippine likely would not have bothered with so many arrangements had Mother Barat not put her in charge and made sure she did it.

The promised six religious became five: Philippine, at forty-eight years, was the oldest and, much against her wishes, was appointed superior of the group. Catherine Lamarre and Marguerite Manteau were thirty-eight. Catherine had made her final profession two years previously, and Marguerite eight years earlier. In the two-tier system in place in many religious orders then, these two were "coadjutrix sisters," who were responsible for domestic duties, as distinct from "choir religious," who served in teaching and leadership roles. The other two companions were considerably younger. Octavie Berthold, age thirty, a convert from Calvinism, had been a novice at Sainte Marie, and so was known to Philippine. She had made her final profession in Paris on February 3, five days before the February 8 departure. Eugénie Audé, age twenty-three, had also been a novice at Sainte Marie and made her final profession at the motherhouse on the morning of departure. She was of a noble family and had been presented at court before becoming a religious. She is the only one of the group known to have expressed a wish to go with Philippine to America.

Some members of Philippine's family were in Paris to see her off, as well as three of the other four missionaries. A member of the community later described the departure. Philippine was dry-eyed, looking straight ahead. At one point, Octavie Berthold hesitated. Philippine gently took her arm and escorted her into the carriage. On the way to the port of Bordeaux, they stopped at Poitiers, where their fifth member, Marguerite Manteau, joined them. But then, in light of the flurry of preparations, it was "hurry up and wait." The weather was not yet seasonable; the ship was not yet ready to leave. They wrote letters, made a retreat—and waited.

Before leaving Paris, Philippine had written a long account of her missionary vocation, which she entrusted to Father Pierre Perreau, a priest friend of the community, to give to Mother Barat after her departure. In it, she recounts the story from her first attraction at the words of a visiting missionary priest at Sainte Marie to her anguish in the last years in Paris when it seemed that she was being called to a way that was impossible to follow. Then, suddenly, the way opened before her. She wrote:

> I value above all else the grace of belonging to the Society of the Heart of Jesus, and that of being able to contribute towards its expansion. No other position in the world could outweigh this heartfelt choice of belonging; at this moment, I am fully aware of

all I owe to the Society and I will try to live up to it and make
the spirit of the Rules of our Society appreciated. To renew often
this holy commitment that, thank God, binds one to the Society,
even at a great distance, will be my consolation.

Sophie read the letter immediately and responded to Philippine four days later, on February 12, as she waited in Bordeaux for the ship to depart:

With great tenderness, dear Mother, I write this first letter, now
that you have accepted your mission—indeed no ordinary mission, for you are leading your little flock so far away from us. The
moment of parting was indeed painful. Long before, the very
thought of it tore my heart; what then was the reality? True, Our
Lord softened our pain by the thought that you would be happy
doing his holy will amidst labor and privation. Moreover, your
example strengthened me, renewing the attraction I had previously had for this vocation. I could not help envying your lot, for
there seems little hope that I would ever share it.…

Father Perreau has given me the papers you confided to
him before you left. As you can imagine, I read them with the
greatest attention. Not that I needed this statement to convince
me that God had called you to this high vocation: the persisting
of your desires, the ease with which the plan, apparently so beset
with difficulties, was finally accomplished when God's time had
come, the way everything concurred to bring about the departure
that cost us so much, and finally the strength God gave you to
overcome obstacles, all this proves to me that in spite of difficulties that in prudence we had to consider, God has called you to
found a house of the Sacred Heart in America.

Finally, on March 19, they boarded the *Rebecca*. By March 21, they had cleared the channel and were on the open sea. The voyage took more than two months and was sometimes rough, with violent storms, seasickness, spoiled food, cramped conditions, and even pirates! By May 16 they had reached the Caribbean. Philippine wrote from Havana about the crossing they had just made:

We have been 52 days seeing nothing but sea and sky; only on May 11 did we sight land from a distance; this was Caicos, the first of the Lucayan Archipelago, which belongs to the English....

That sea is terrible; at certain moments I thought of writing to you to beg you not to send anyone else before receiving more precise news of us and being assured of the worth of so much sacrifice.... A storm at sea is a truly terrifying spectacle. The noise from the breaking waves and roaring wind would drown any thunder or cannonade. It is absolutely deafening, and added to that is the rolling of the vessel itself. The sailors shout to encourage one another in their work; it is a lugubrious sound, but their silence is more dismal and still worse is the sight of the captain pacing the deck in an anxious mood. The ship tossing violently in an angry sea gives the impression of the confusion of the last day. The sky seems to roll up rapidly behind the mountains of water, dragging the stars with it. The sea, nearly black in the storm, constantly gapes wide, disclosing bottomless depths; the waves sweep over the deck as the ship rolls and pitches. Twice the waves have forced open our little portholes and drenched our beds at night. The masts bend, the sails are furled or torn; the helm is abandoned in order not to strain the vessel. All this is no laughing matter unless one sees God in the storm.

It was still weeks before the weary passengers disembarked in the middle of the night at New Orleans on May 29, Feast of the Sacred Heart that year. It was dark when, for the first time since March 19, they set foot on land. Philippine knelt quickly and kissed the ground. "You do it, too," she said to the others. "No one is watching." As soon as it was light, they arrived by carriage at the Ursuline Convent, situated near the Saint Louis Cathedral in what is now known as the French Quarter. Philippine and her companions had been expected and were welcomed with open arms. They were overwhelmed with the generous hospitality of the Ursuline Sisters, who had been in the city since 1727, almost

Old Ursuline Covent, New Orleans

a century, and who provided everything for them. Philippine had expected word from Bishop Dubourg when she arrived, but there was nothing.

In New Orleans, Philippine caught her first glimpses of Native Americans and had her first encounter with slavery, which she found too incredible to accept. "Can this be?" she wrote in a letter to Mother Josephine Bigeu the day after arrival, May 30, 1818. "The civil law that makes them free is not observed except in a small part of the United States." Within a few days, however, she became involved with the blacks and in little more than a week, she was thinking about how to provide the service of education to all racial groups.

Philippine was also disillusioned by the state of the church in this thriving port city. Her idealism had led her to expect nothing but saints. Instead, she heard sermons of doubtful theology by one priest—sermons she said would never have been accepted in France. The cathedral was under the sway of Capuchin Father Antonio de Sedella, venerated as a saint by many and vilified by others, but immensely loved by his parishioners. He refused either to cede the cathedral or to accept the authority of Bishop Dubourg and his vicar, Father Louis Sibourd.

Still, in spite of having acquired scurvy on the sea voyage, Philippine was brimming with energy and excitement, even exclaiming to Father Varin only four days after arriving that her thoughts "have raced to the far northwest and across the South Sea to Korea or Japan to gain the martyr's palm. That is the way with ambition in this world—never satisfied. But I can assure you that mine would stop there, and after martyrdom I will want nothing."

Despite Philippine's generally penitential approach regarding even modest luxuries, she learned to make adjustments for her health in her new environment.

Mother Girard would laugh to see me every morning take not only a little coffee without sugar covertly, but a large cup of coffee au lait sugared like syrup. Seeing that I did not want to eat breakfast, the superior had me ordered to do so by the doctor, who says it is absolutely necessary here, and it would be rather better not to eat supper. So this is what I do.

(Letter from New Orleans to Mother de Gramont in Paris, June 1818)

After six weeks in New Orleans to recover from the voyage, during which the religious wrote interesting observations back to France, they began on July 12 a long trip of another forty days on the steamboat *Franklin* up the Mississippi River to Saint Louis. Steamboats had been plying the Mississippi only since 1811, and the journey was still a perilous one. Happily, this time, the *Franklin* made the trip safely, despite the inconvenience of being grounded on a sandbar for nineteen hours.

In her first weeks and months in America, Philippine was always looking for ways to give accounts of her new home to those she had left, religious and students. She used her well-developed powers of observation to record what she saw and heard. In letters and reports, she describes plants, flowers, animals, and settlements as she sees and is told about them, some of it fanciful, but nevertheless making fascinating reading for her far-away audience. Some of her descriptions for the students could almost have served as biology lessons.

At half the distance to New Orleans, the woods are no longer only undergrowth, but they are good timber trees: the green oak, the sycamore, thorns, high poplars and willows. Along the water are enormous palm trees whose leaves are very large, and when tied together by the stems, they make a large fan. These leaves make brooms, adorn the loveliest straw hats, and are used by the Indians to make their baskets. They paint them with different designs to make them in the manner that you will see. The Mexican Indians are natural artists and make very beautiful things of shells.

To finish what I want to tell you about the banks of the Mississippi, the part in the neighborhood of New Orleans is cleared of these trees that good cultivation will not replace. The marshy areas are not right for good vegetation. Vines die and dry up, cherries and currants do not produce fruit, the best plums are like our worst, peaches rot, and vegetables are very expensive. Figs and oranges do well, but this winter that was extremely cold for this region made many oranges die, and in the best years, they do not compare to those of Cuba. They gave us some en route, much better than those of France, with pineapple and bananas. Cuba also exports tobacco and sugar cane, which cannot mature to have their full sweetness; we eat it raw here; the refined kind comes from France and is also expensive. (Letter to the students in Paris and Grenoble, June 3, 1818)

5

TO SAINT CHARLES ON THE MISSOURI

THE SAINT LOUIS to which the five religious came on August 22 had been founded in 1764 by French fur traders Jean-Pierre Laclede and René-Auguste Chouteau at a strategic location on the Mississippi River, near its junction with the Missouri. It quickly became a major center of the fur trade to the north and west. Once arrived in Saint Louis, the nuns received hospitality for a short time from the Bernard Pratte family. General Bernard Pratte, along with Pierre Chouteau, was among the wealthiest residents of the city. The two men were major agents of the booming fur trade that came down the Missouri River and, although Philippine did not write about it, it is probable that in the summer of 1818, while staying at the Pratte house, she met William Clark of the famous Lewis and Clark Expedition of 1804-1806 and now Governor of the Missouri Territory.

It had been Mother Barat's wish, and the understanding of the religious making the journey, that they would be established in Saint Louis. However, unable to find a suitable house for them there, Bishop Dubourg sent them west to Saint Charles, a small town on the Missouri River about twenty-five miles away. It had been founded for the fur trade by Louis Blanchette in 1769, under the name Les Petites Côtes (The Little Hills) It was so named because of its location nestled between the Missouri River and a rise of small hills behind. (Under Spanish control, from 1762 to 1800, it was renamed San Carlos Borromeo.) The religious arrived in Saint Charles on September 7, 1818, and were welcomed to their new home, the "Duquette Mansion." Rented from the widow of François Duquette, it was situated on ground slightly above the level of the Missouri River and the town spread out below. The house had seven rooms, one large one across the front, and three smaller ones behind, on either side off a central corridor. The house was dedicated to Saint Francis Regis, according to a vow Philippine had made in France.

Duquette House

A week later, on September 14, 1818, the religious opened the free school, the first Sacred Heart School in the New World, and a short time later, on October 3, three boarders arrived to open the boarding school. The first boarders were Emilie and Therese Pratte, daughters of the nuns' Saint Louis host, Bernard Pratte, and their cousin, Pelagie Chouteau, daughter of another prominent Saint Louis family.

Since childhood Philippine had dreamed of going to educate and convert the native people in America known in France as *les sauvages*. But like many romantic dreams, it was to be fulfilled in a reality quite different from what she had imagined. When Philippine and her companions arrived in Missouri, the population was nearly all French and Catholic, but the westward movement of Protestant Americans from the East was well underway. Moreover, the land in which she was to spend the rest of her life had been sold to the United States government in the Louisiana Purchase of 1803. Then, just three years after Philippine's arrival, in 1821, Missouri was admitted to the Union as a state where slavery was legal. This was done to balance the simultaneous admission of Maine as a free state.

So now, almost immediately after their arrival, Philippine and her companions found themselves living, not in a French colorny, or even in newly American territory, but within the United States, something they had not expected. No evidence exists, however, that Philippine or any of her first companions ever became American citizens. They most likely remained citizens of France.

From the beginning, the religious all realized how important it was to learn English in this rapidly changing land. Octavie Berthold was said to already be fluent in Latin, Italian, and English. The others studied English before departing and along the way. Eugénie learned English well enough, though Philippine wrote that the Americans found her accent hard to understand. For

Philippine, who lacked a gift for languages, English was a lifelong trial. Over the years, she learned to read and understand it, but despite many occasions in which she did have to speak it, she never considered herself capable of speaking it fluently.

Isolated in Saint Charles, the missionary band suffered acutely from lack of communication with the outside. Letters were slow to arrive and sometimes lost. Months went by with little communication with the home they had left behind. For Philippine, another trial was the expectation that she serve as religious superior, simply because she was the oldest and the obvious choice. Although she had amazing powers of observation and was a good writer, she was inexperienced in this kind of leadership and did not know how best to guide or give account of the religious under her charge. In these new situations of stress, she could often be critical rather than understanding. She was critical as well of many of the Americans she met, whom she considered to be lovers of independence and luxury.

Another major adjustment for the missionaries was adapting to a culture in which the norms of social status from the Old World would not hold. All free persons considered themselves to be social equals, yet ironically there was slavery, the greatest social inequality. The fact that the new state of Missouri had been admitted to the Union as a state in which slavery could continue created difficulty for the religious, who did not want slaves. Yet, as Philippine wrote in a letter to her cousin Josephine on August 27, 1820, they had discovered that most whites would not do the sort of domestic work they needed done.

Despite her distaste for slavery, Philippine was not immune to the negative white stereotypes of enslaved persons and repeated them occasionally in her letters. Within a short time, though, she indicated she had been thinking of some way to bring black women into religious life. In a letter to Mother Barat on November 15, 1819, she suggested a kind of "third order" of extern sisters, recognizing the impossibility of incorporating blacks into the white community at that time. Although her idea could not be realized, and black children could not be accepted into the boarding or day school, the religious gave them a basic education whenever possible. A little more than a decade later, Philippine would again raise the question of a special order with Bishop Rosati in a letter dated April 11, 1831. But nothing seems to have come of her proposals.

This tension between equality and inequality was evident even within the community of nuns, who continued to distinguish between choir religious and coadjutrix sisters. The difference was quite visible, as they wore slightly different habits. Already in 1819, Bishop Dubourg had told the missionaries that having two classes of sisters would not work on the American frontier. Philippine tenaciously clung to the tradition, however, knowing that was the way it was done in France with its regulated social hierarchy. The religious also needed to adjust their ideas of cloister, which was simply impossible to maintain in the New World. Even though they stayed at home, they had little choice but to receive many curious visitors.

Protestant churches abounded in the frontier setting, and true to their counter-Reformation European background, the little group of nuns considered Protestant churches to be heretical. Yet they accepted Protestant children in their schools, hoping of course to convert them. They felt a strong competition with Protestant missionaries who were often more successful at gaining converts. Even though the missionaries were imbued with a spirituality of love through their formation in devotion to the Sacred Heart, elements of Jansenism, the rigid religious movement that had taken hold in France, remained. Philippine's eagerness for sacramental confession when she had hardly any opportunity to sin seems strange to us. In reality, though, confession could be a means to personal spiritual direction, which was sorely needed by these women thrust into a strange land. Yet the constant fear of not responding to grace was deeply felt, keeping Philippine and others like her in deep self-doubt, when a more affirming spirituality might have been more helpful. While strong female spiritual leaders such as Sophie Barat were able to exercise some spiritual guidance, in the Catholic Church of the nineteenth century, priests were considered the authoritative religious experts because of their education and ordination. Still, the priests did not always welcome the obligations of the pastoral care of nuns. It must have seemed painfully awkward on both sides at times to receive the only spiritual advice available under the sacrament of confession from the same men with whom the nuns would have to negotiate business affairs.

6

TO FLORISSANT IN THE COUNTRY

BISHOP DUBOURG, though courageous and bold, was not a realistic manager, and he made arbitrary decisions that affected the nuns' welfare. Only a year after settling them in Saint Charles, he found land for them at Saint Ferdinand in Florissant, on the east side of the Missouri, closer to Saint Louis, and insisted that they uproot and move again. Because of the bishop's insistence, the religious had no choice but to move in September 1819, before the beginning of classes, though the house would still take another three months to be completed. They lived temporarily—and conducted a school—in an old farm building on the bishop's property.

The house at Saint Ferdinand was not ready for them to move into until late December. The final move took place in cold and snow on the days just before Christmas. In her letters, Philippine describes trying to lead the cows in heavy snow, dropping her bag of valuables, including her watch, and having to search for it in piles of snow. The first Mass in the new convent was Midnight Mass on Christmas Eve, 1819. By 1820, the boarding school counted seventeen girls, who together wrote to Mother Barat in France to congratulate her for her feast day. The same year, a novitiate was opened at Florissant. It began almost immediately to prosper. By 1821 there were six novices, three of them from among the seventeen students who had written to Mother Barat the year before. In August of the same year, Philippine was looking to the horizon once more, writing to Sophie that she longed to go to Peru—but she knew this time that Florissant would be home for quite a while.

There was the need to set up a new shrine of Saint Francis Regis in the new church, in fulfillment of Philippine's vow. In 1821, Bishop Dubourg gave Philippine a very large painting of the death of Saint Francis Regis. It was proudly hung in the nuns' chapel at Florissant, where it remained until 1840, when Mother Galitzine, no longer understanding the reason for the shrine, ordered it dismantled. It remained in storage until 1847, when it was brought to the school in Saint Charles, where it resides today.

Death of John Francis Regis
Academy of the Sacred Heart, Saint Charles, Missouri, Artist Unknown

Only three years after the missionaries' arrival in Missouri, in 1821, they would return to Louisiana, to a small town up the Mississippi River called Grand Coteau or Opelousas, where the widow Mrs. Smith was offering land and a house. This meant splitting the little band of five who had come together across the sea, even though a flow of new American vocations had already begun and other missionaries were promised from France. So on August 5, 1821, Mother Eugénie Audé and the novice Mary Layton boarded a steamboat for Louisiana to found the second Sacred Heart community and school in America. When two new nuns arrived from France early the next year, one, Xavier Murphy, went to Opelousas where she would become superior four years later, when Eugénie struck out for yet another new foundation at Saint Michael, Louisiana. Lucile Mathevon, the other new arrival, traveled north to Saint Louis. She would later be the refounder of Saint Charles in 1828, and eventually leader of the pioneer band to the Native American mission at Sugar Creek in 1841.

Original House, Grand Coteau, Louisiana

Archive photo

7

FIRST VISIT TO LOUISIANA

UPON DEPARTURE FROM FRANCE IN 1818, Philippine had been named superior and, because of the distance, given certain powers over new foundations that superiors would not normally have had. The new foundation at Grand Coteau, deftly led by the gracious Mother Eugénie Audé, began to flourish quickly. The year after the nuns went south, in 1822, Philippine decided to make the long journey down the Mississippi to visit the new house in Louisiana. With her was Therese Pratte, a Florissant student and daughter of the Pratte family, in whose house the original group had stayed when they first arrived in Saint Louis. She longed to see again her beloved Mother Eugénie and then return to Saint Louis with Mother Duchesne.

When the religious first went up the Mississippi River from New Orleans to Saint Louis in 1818, steamboat travel was very new—the latest thing—and the journey took six weeks. This time, four years later, the steamboat journey downstream to disembarkation at Plaquemine took only seventeen days. But then came the tortuous travel by rowboat through the Louisiana bayous to Grand Coteau.

The visit itself went without incident. One of the boarding students in the school was Mary Ann Hardey, who read an address of welcome in French for the distinguished visitor. Later, as Mother Aloysia Hardey (1809-1886), she would lead foundations in the eastern United States, Canada and Cuba, and become the first American assistant general at the motherhouse in Paris in 1872.

The return to Saint Louis was catastrophic. Philippine and Therese Pratte, the student traveling with her, went to New Orleans to board the steamboat *Hecla* there for the journey back up the Mississippi. They had been assured there was no yellow fever in New Orleans, but by the time they arrived, a serious outbreak had occurred. Philippine contracted it before boarding the steamboat north. On the second day, three people on the boat died, including the captain and first mate! Philippine and Therese had to disembark at Natchez, where they were given hospitality by a local family. Only after nearly three months were they able to return home to Saint Louis on the steamboat *Cincinnati*.

Philippine returned to her life at Florissant with the small community, a growing number of novices, and a farm that in 1823 included seven cows and sixty chickens. Throughout these years, there are frequent references to a foundation in New Orleans, but for various reasons, it never came about. Instead, another foundation was made by Eugénie Audé in 1825 at a location closer to that city, along the banks of the Mississippi at Saint Michael. Eugénie was highly successful wherever she went, and began to assume relative independence with regard to the authority of Philippine, who habitually compared herself unfavorably to others. There was thought of Philippine's moving south to one of the Louisiana houses because they were doing so well, but she was firmly against it. Florissant was poor and she liked it that way.

Original Building, Saint Michael, Louisiana, 1825

An added attraction of Florissant was the arrival of the Jesuits in 1823. Bishop Dubourg hoped to set up in Missouri a school for Native Americans and a seminary for the training of future missionaries. For this purpose, the bishop offered the Jesuits a valuable tract of land that he owned. The Jesuit contingent arrived from Maryland in May 1823: two priests, three lay brothers, seven young Belgian novices, and three young black couples, all under the leadership of Father Charles Felix Van Quickenborne. Among the novices, who had come to Maryland in 1821 to be trained for the American mission, were two who would play historically significant roles in the region. One was Peter J. Verhaegen, who would later be the priest to insist that Philippine be included in the missionary band to Sugar Creek, and the pastor who presided at her funeral in Saint Charles when she died in 1852. The other was Peter Jan De Smet, who would become the famous missionary to the West. Philippine and the rest of her community at Florissant were elated by this sudden appearance of the Jesuit spiritual support to which they had been accustomed in France, even if the notoriously harsh Van Quickenborne and Philippine regularly clashed. It was he who, as a result of a disagreement between them one year, forbade Philippine in the confessional to receive Communion on the coming Feast of the Sacred Heart, thereby preventing her from renewing her vows with the community. She did the only thing she could think of to avoid the scandal of the superior not receiving Communion and renewing her vows: she pretended to be sick and stayed in bed all day.

By 1825, Philippine seemed preoccupied about death and how to provide for those around her if she died. This may have been because the state of medical practice was primitive and she was witnessing so much death around her. She did not die, however, but left her dear Florissant in 1827 to begin a fourth foundation, this time finally in Saint Louis itself, thanks to the benefaction of John Mullanphy. A successful Irish immigrant, Mullanphy was one of the wealthiest men in the city and a patron of social works for the needy. One of the conditions for his gift of the land and house to the Society of the Sacred Heart was that the school also provide for up to twenty orphan girls, to be selected by himself or his daughters. According to the agreement, he or later his heirs, would provide ten dollars for each girl upon entrance and five dollars each year following, an amount that even in those days did not suffice. The rest had to be made up by the income of the house or other donations. Mullanphy continued to be mindful of the poor of the city, however. The next year, he also established the first hospital in Saint Louis, staffed by the Sisters of Charity. The new boarding school at the City House opened on September 17, 1827. His granddaughter, Ann Biddle Chambers Thatcher (1828-1913), would later give testimony in 1900 for the cause of beatification of Philippine. The work of the orphanage at the City House would continue until 1947.

8

DEPARTURE OF BISHOP DUBOURG AND RETURN TO SAINT CHARLES

BISHOP DUBOURG, increasingly besieged by problems and opposition, finally had had enough of frontier life. He visited Saint Louis one last time in 1826 before departing for France, where he resigned his episcopal appointment. He had said nothing about a resignation before he left, so the news came as a great surprise. His coadjutor, Joseph Rosati, an Italian Vincentian priest, earlier recruited and highly trusted by Dubourg, was immediately appointed apostolic administrator of the diocese. Before his consecration as bishop, however, the diocese was divided, and he became the first bishop of Saint Louis in March 1827, while remaining apostolic administrator of the new diocese of New Orleans until 1829. Rosati remained bishop of Saint Louis throughout the time that Philippine held the office of superior. Their relationship was a close one, and she had recourse to him frequently. One hundred forty-eight of her letters to him are extant.

In the intervening years, since the abandonment of the first house in Saint Charles in 1819, there had been frequent negotiations with residents who wanted the religious to return, and with the Jesuits who were building a stone church on the same property.

In 1828, the community at Saint Charles was reopened by Lucile Mathevon and Mary Ann O'Connor, and the school opened on October 10. They continued to live and operate their school in the old Duquette building until 1835, when a new building was built farther down the hill. The Duquette house continued in use until 1858.

Meanwhile in the South, yet a third house was founded in Louisiana at La Fourche, west of New Orleans, by Hélène Dutour, who had arrived from France the year before. The Society was experiencing amazing growth in its new American home. Just ten years after the first arrival, there were now six houses of the Sacred Heart in America, three in the south and three in Missouri. The number of religious had increased to twenty-seven, only eleven of whom had come from Europe. Plus there were twenty-five American novices.

The lack of privacy and American resistance to social distinctions among religious and students continued to present difficulties. The model imported from France was of paying boarding students from the elite classes (*pensionnat*) and free day schools for the poor (*école gratuite*). In between the two distinct classes, schools for paying day students from the emerging middle classes (*externat*) were being established, but this new model was often resisted by those of a traditional mindset who did not realize the changing social reality. The new model of paying day students began to be implemented in America as well. The question of paying day students had been unsettled until now. Many parents who could afford to pay wanted Sacred Heart education for their daughters but were not willing to consign them to the complete and nearly year-long seclusion of the boarding school. Parents of the boarding students also pressured for more access to their daughters. Philippine resisted, regarding the total convent environment to be ideal for character formation and, in her letters, often lamented the negative effect of contact with families and home visits on the boarding students.

In addition to boarding school and day school, at Florissant they had tried to establish a small school for Native American girls, beginning in 1825, at the same time that the Jesuits began their school for Native American boys. The attempts lasted only two years. The Native American children did not want to be there, far from their families, and found it impossible to sit still for long periods in the European manner. They frequently ran away. At Saint Louis, there were boarding students, day students, and the orphanage. In every case, each group was intended to remain separate from the others for instruction and care. With such small groups and close quarters, it is difficult to imagine how that was done.

9

SECOND JOURNEY TO LOUISIANA, 1829

BY 1829, there were tensions among the three Louisiana houses, which competed for personnel and students. Mother Barat asked Mother Duchesne to make the trip south once more to convoke a council of the three Louisiana superiors, Mothers Eugénie Audé of Saint Michael, Xavier Murphy of Grand Coteau, and Hélène Dutour of La Fourche. Mother Barat directed Philippine to preside and to try to settle some difficulties with regard to the aims of the respective schools and potential competition among them. This time, travel in both directions went smoothly, but the outcome of the visit was ambiguous. Mother Duchesne conferred with the three superiors at Saint Michael, but the diffident Philippine was no match for three lively women, each defending her own turf. Before leaving Louisiana, she visited the other two houses as well. A little over three months after setting off from Saint Louis, she had returned safely, but nothing was accomplished by her journey. Saint Michael, under the direction of Mother Audé, continued to flourish, as did Grand Coteau under the direction of the Irish born Xavier Murphy. La Fourche, beset with accumulated problems and debts, would close in 1832.

Eugénie Audé was already in the habit of ignoring Philippine's authority, even though Philippine was nominally her superior. Rather, she went straight to Mother Barat. She now went so far as telling Mother Barat that Philippine was not fit to be superior—a point that Philippine herself had been making for years. It was clear that the Saint Louis houses were not flourishing like the Louisiana ones. In a letter to Philippine dated October 31, 1831, Sophie raised the idea of merging Florissant and the City House, but Bishop Rosati was not in favor and the idea was dropped.

Mother Barat seemed also to have been getting complaints from some of the religious in Saint Louis. This time she tried to acquiesce and remove Philippine from office. Her letter to Philippine of November 30, 1831, must have elated its recipient. The letter alludes to complaints Mother Barat had received about order, the quality of education, and even cleanliness, all said in the kindly way of, "Heaven knows I don't blame you, dear Mother, but it's getting to be too much for you."[1] However, when Bishop Rosati was informed, he would not hear of it. Rather, he wrote a very strong letter to Mother Barat in which he praised Philippine as one widely respected, whom no one could replace, who had done all that could be done, and who was not to be blamed for lack of success—quite the contrary of what others, even Philippine herself, had been telling Mother Barat, who had to accede to the bishop's wishes, and Philippine remained superior at the City House.

---

1. This letter of Madeleine Sophie Barat to Philippine contains the famous statement of Mother Barat that is often quoted, most frequently out of context: Times change and we must change, too, and modify our views.

10

TIMES OF EXPANSION AND LOSS

THE PERIOD OF RAPID GROWTH in members continued. By 1830, the Society in Missouri and Louisiana counted
forty-five vowed religious, only fourteen of whom were from
Europe, and twenty-three novices. This growth of the Society
of the Sacred Heart in America parallels the overall growth of
population in the central region of the continent. During these
years, the rapid increase of English-speaking Americans from
the East, followed by German and then Irish immigrants, was
changing the character of the land to which the missionaries
had come. English was more and more necessary, and Philippine never felt confident using it. This created a gap between
her and both students and religious who knew no French,
making her feel still more useless in spite of the obvious success
of the works.

On September 16, 1833, Octavie Berthold died in Philippine's
community in Saint Louis at the age of forty-six, the first of the
original band of missionaries to die. She had suffered courageously
for some years with what seems to have been a cancer of the throat.
It was a sobering moment for Philippine. Perhaps it was the reason
that during these years, she often turned to the thought of death in

her letters to Mother Barat. Yet, despite all this concern, she would live another nineteen years and see all of her original companions die before her.

11

RETURN TO FLORISSANT

IN 1834, PHILIPPINE RETURNED to her beloved Saint Ferdinand in Florissant, still as superior. During these years, she asked in nearly every letter to Sophie Barat to be relieved of that office, which she had never wanted and in which she continually found herself to compare unfavorably with others whom she saw as more successful in leadership.

At the General Council of the Society in November 1833 in France, Eugénie Audé was elected, *in absentia* after consultation with the religious in America, assistant general for America, with instructions to visit all the houses and then return to France to give an account. This news did not reach Saint Louis until March 1834. In April, Mother Audé passed through Saint Louis on her way to France, but in October 1836, Mother Barat wrote that they should no longer expect Eugénie to return because of her failing health. She died on March 6, 1842, at the age of fifty-one, as superior at the Trinità dei Monti in Rome, while Philippine was finally realizing her dream of living among Native Americans.

Finally in 1840, Elizabeth Galitzine, visitator general from Paris, relieved Philippine of the office of superior, which she had held for twenty-two years. *The Journal of the Society in America,* which she had kept faithfully since their arrival in 1818, ceased to be kept by her. She retired from Florissant to the City House in Saint Louis, now a simple but revered senior member of the community.

12

THE DREAM COMES TRUE

THOUGH SEVENTY-ONE YEARS OLD, Philippine was finally free to pursue what she had thought would be her life's work. She was more and more excited about the possibilities of going west to the frontier where she would be able to fulfill her whole purpose for having come to America, a purpose thus far continually thwarted by the necessity of building solid foundations in the rapidly developing centers of American frontier expansion.

Father Peter Verhaegen, S.J., had arrived in Saint Louis asking for sisters to join the Jesuit mission with the Potawatomi at Sugar Creek, Kansas. In September 1838, more than 800 native men, women and children had been placed under military control and marched from Indiana to Kansas on the "Trail of Death." More than forty of the weak and elderly had died. In 1841, four Religious of the Sacred Heart answered Father Verhaegen's call to the Native American mission. Philippine was thought to be so frail that she could die any day, but at the thought of going, her energy returned. The story of her inclusion in the band destined to go, as recounted by Lucile Mathevon, is touching. The group of religious was sitting in the City House parlor with Father Verhaegen discussing the project, when he suddenly realized that Philippine had not been included in the plans. He insisted that she was going —even if they had to carry her.

The four Religious of the Sacred Heart set out with Father Verhaegen from Saint Louis on June 29, 1841. Besides Philippine, they were Mothers Lucile Mathevon and Mary Ann O'Connor, both from Saint Charles, and Louise Amyot (or Amyotte) from the City House in Saint Louis. All three would die at the Native American mission years later. Philippine hoped to die there, too.

In just a few days they had arrived at "the land of our desires" as Philippine wrote to Madeleine Sophie later in July. Philippine's elation at being there was soon tempered by her inability to learn the difficult language, even as she watched some of her companions pick up some of it rather quickly. While in Sugar Creek, she would have received news of the death of Marguerite Manteau, the second of her original companions to die, on July 4, 1841, age sixty-two, at Grand Coteau, and perhaps the news had also reached her there of the death of Eugénie Audé, her third original companion, on March 6, 1842. Now, of the five who made the original journey, only Philippine and Catherine Lamarre remained.

Life at Sugar Creek was incredibly harsh, yet Philippine relished it. She could not communicate with the Native Americans, but they revered her for her long hours of prayer, calling her "the woman who is always praying," and would come reverently to kiss the hem of her habit. While Philippine wrote that she was invigorated by her new adventure and looking to go still farther west, the other nuns were very apprehensive about her health in such rugged conditions. The superior, Lucile Mathevon, worried about her incessantly. Visitator Mother Elizabeth Galitzine came for a brief visit in the spring and reported back on Philippine's frail health. The new Bishop Kenrick, replacing Bishop Rosati who had been assigned a new mission in 1840, paid a visit to Sugar Creek and tried to convince her to return to Saint Louis. After reports from both Mothers Galitzine and Mathevon, Mother Barat agreed. No letter of Madeleine Sophie to Philippine at that time is extant, but one to Lucile Mathevon, superior of the mission, dated April 16, 1842, advises that it would be better for Philippine to return to Saint Charles, or wherever else she wished to go, and another to Regis Hamilton, superior at Saint Charles, dated April 18, requests that she write to Philippine to invite her there.

So it was that on June 19, 1842, just short of a year since their arrival at Sugar Creek, Father Verhaegen escorted Philippine back to Saint Charles, where she was welcomed by the community. It was to be her final place of residence.

13

WHEN THE GRAIN OF WHEAT FALLS TO THE GROUND

THE FINAL YEARS (1842-1852)

A COMMON IMAGE OF PHILIPPINE during those final ten years is of an old woman quietly praying in the corner. That is not quite accurate. Indeed she did spend long hours in prayer, but she was also engaged in numerous activities. During these last years of her life in Saint Charles, the Society in America expanded to New York, Pennsylvania, Detroit and Montreal. Philippine stayed well informed about the new foundations in America, as well as in Europe, and wrote to her friends there. She read assiduously the *Annals of the Society for the Propagation of the Faith* and received frequent visits from returning missionaries like Father De Smet, who sometimes brought her Native American girls to care for. She was very involved with the students in the school, many of whom remembered stories about her fifty years later when asked to testify to her holiness. For several years she is listed in the Society catalog as teacher in the parish day school, an interesting fact in view of the general impression that her English was poor. Remembrances survived much later of plays she wrote for the children and sewing that she did for sick children. The little museum in Saint Charles holds items she made for the children, such as doll furniture.

She was always good with a needle, and when her eyes could no longer thread it, she called in a student or two to do it for her. Her correspondence indicates that she was actively involved in making vestments for a number of priests. She composed several lists of important events in the Society and the American mission, perhaps as an exercise in memory retention. She continued many of her ongoing relationships with family, friends, and former novices. On July 5, 1845, she received the news of the death of Catherine Lamarre at Florissant at the age of sixty-six, the last of the original band of missionaries except for Philippine, who, though the oldest of the group, would be the one to outlive them all.

During the years 1846-1847, there was a puzzling nearly two-year silence between Philippine and Madeleine Sophie. There are many possible reasons to account for it. Since Philippine was no longer superior, she did not need to give an account to the Mother General, and a recommendation had gone out to refrain from writing unnecessarily to Mother Barat because of her burden of work. Letters were sometimes also lost in transit. When Philippine wrote in June 1846, pleading for the survival of the house at Florissant, her plea went unheeded, so perhaps she felt after that that it was pointless to write. Mother Barat was indeed overburdened with the task of correspondence and government during those years, and possibly simply forgot to write to an old friend with whom she no longer needed to conduct business. Whatever the cause, Philippine felt it keenly. Her trusted friend Regis Hamilton, who had welcomed her to Saint Charles in 1842, was taken away in 1847 to serve as superior in Saint-Jacques, Canada, then Eden Hall in Philadelphia, then Detroit. During those years Philippine was living under a superior, Emilie St-Cyr, who had formerly been her novice. She had been appointed by Mother Galitzine but, in Philippine's view, had no gifts for governance.

The silence with Madeleine Sophie broke on September 8, 1847, with the arrival of a special visitor—Philippine's niece, Amelie (Aloysia) Jouve, now a Religious of the Sacred Heart on her way to mission in Canada. Sophie had instructed Aloysia to go from France to Canada by way of Saint Louis to visit her aunt, whom she would not have seen since 1818. Aloysia spent two weeks with Philippine. She brought a letter from Mother Barat, no longer extant, but alluded to in Philippine's response two days later, on September 10, 1847. Philippine was overjoyed to receive this letter, and exclaimed her joy that Mother Barat still remembered her. When Aloysia asked her aunt if there was anything she could do for her, Philippine had two requests: to recover the large painting of the death of Saint Francis Regis, given to her by Bishop Dubourg in 1821, from the storage at Saint Ferdinand to which it had been relegated, and to bring back Regis Hamilton, then serving in Canada, to again be superior at Saint Charles. The painting was brought to Saint Charles, where it remains today, and Regis Hamilton returned as superior at Saint Charles, but not until November 1851, one year before Philippine's death. The correspondence between the two friends resumed. Seven more letters from Philippine to Madeleine Sophie are extant from the period before her death on November 18, 1852, and two from Madeleine Sophie to Philippine, in December 1849 and February 1852.

On November 8, 1850, news reached Philippine of the death on September 23 of her beloved cousin and best friend, Josephine Perier de Savoye-Rollin in France, at the age of eighty. "Mother of the poor and my closest friend," she wrote the next day. Her contemporaries were dying. She still remained.

14

TO HEAVEN AND BEYOND

PHILIPPINE GRADUALLY WEAKENED, and her death came as the noon angelus was ringing on November 18, 1852. Two days before her death, Philippine had a visitor: Mother Anna du Rousier, visitator general from Paris, who had been sent to make a visit of all the American houses. It was a cold rainy day and Mother du Rousier was not well, but knowing that Philippine's time was running out, she insisted on making the journey from Saint Louis. She found Philippine very weak, but in response to a request for a blessing, Philippine traced a cross on her forehead. "I can still feel that cross," wrote Mother du Rousier sometime later. Oral tradition has it that they exchanged profession crosses. Unknown at the time to either of them was that Mother du Rousier would in the next year be the foundress of a new foundation in Chile, and later, one in Peru, where, according to the tradition, she wore Philippine's profession cross until her death.[2]

Father Peter Verhaegen, S.J., the same dear friend who had insisted that Philippine come on the mission to Kansas, and had

---

2. According to the same oral tradition, the cross was then taken to the motherhouse and given by Superior General Mabel Digby to Janet Erskine Stuart, who wore it until her death. Today it is kept in the Society's general archives in Rome.

brought her back to Saint Charles a year later, was, at the time of her death, pastor of the Jesuit parish of Saint Charles Borromeo, situated next door to the convent in Saint Charles. Thus, Father Verhaegen became the priest who performed Philippine's funeral and burial in the convent cemetery. In the parish register, he wrote:

> On the 20th of November, 1852, I, the undersigned, buried the mortal remains of Madame Philippine Duchesne, professed religious of the Society of the Sacred Heart, aged 83 years.
>
> Madame Duchesne was a native of France, and came to the United States of America with a small number of religious of the Society of the Sacred Heart in 1818. She may be considered the foundress of all the houses of the Sacred Heart in the United States. Eminent in all virtues of religious life, but especially in humility, she sweetly and calmly departed this life in the odor of sanctity on the 18th day of November, 1852.
>
> [signed] P. J. Verhaegen, S.J.

A few days later, Mother du Rousier wrote from Saint Louis:

> It is the general opinion here that we have lost a saint. The clergy, and the Archbishop in particular, speak of her with the greatest admiration. Archbishop Kenrick declared she was the noblest and most virtuous soul he had ever known. Father De Smet says that while living she was worthy of canonization. Our American houses owe everything to her.

The entry for her funeral in the house journal of the community concludes: "We had her daguerreotype taken in case she may one day be canonized."

That expectation began to be fulfilled when, about the year 1900, testimonies began to be collected from elderly women who had known Philippine as children, and from others who could testify to her heroic virtue. After examination of the life and virtues of Mother Duchesne, the Vatican's Sacred Congregation for Rites (now Congregation for the Causes of Saints) pronounced her "Venerable," which meant that the cause could continue and she could be held in veneration. According to the canonization process of the Catholic Church, two documented miraculous healings are required for the next step, beatification; that is, declaring the holy person "blessed."

In Rome in late October 1930, Mother Caroline Indelli, RSCJ, was suffering acutely from a chronic mastoid infection in the left ear. There had been two surgeries with no improvement. During a novena made by the community for her healing, on November 3, the entire wound was suddenly healed. When the doctor saw it on November 10, he declared that no known science could explain the sudden healing. This was accepted as the first miracle.

In late December of 1931, Francisco Bahamonde, a maintenance worker at the convent and school of the Sacred Heart in Ponce, Puerto Rico, was dying of cirrhosis of the liver. On January 6, 1932, his wife sent word to the convent that he was in his final moments. The religious sent a relic of Mother Duchesne and instructed his wife to place it on his liver. On the morning of January 7, he was completely healed. This was accepted as the second miracle attributed to Mother Duchesne.

The acceptance of these two miracles paved the way for the beatification of Philippine, which took place in Rome on May 12, 1940. Soon after the event, the Archdiocese of Saint Louis began to plan for the erection of a shrine in her honor on the grounds of the Academy of the Sacred Heart in Saint Charles, Missouri.

Ground was broken in April 1951, and the first phase of the building was completed in 1952, with solemn dedication and transfer of Mother Duchesne's sarcophagus to the new church on June 11. The original plan was for the building to be cruciform, with the addition of the nave to come later. In time, however, it was decided to keep the church in the shape in which it was first built. The interior was redesigned by William Schickel in 1967 into the style that it bears today.

Shrine of St. Philippine in Saint Charles, Missouri
Renovation by William Schickel, 1967

Death photo of Philippine Duchesne, 1852

One more miracle was needed for canonization, that is, to have Mother Duchesne officially declared a saint of the Catholic Church. Mother Marguerite Bernard, RSCJ, had lived for many years in China, and with the rest of the religious, had to leave the country at the time of the Communist takeover in 1949-1950. After spending some time in Tokyo, she arrived in San Francisco very ill with thyroid cancer. Medical examination determined the tumor to be inoperable. Prayers were said through the intercession of Mother Duchesne, and Mother Bernard did not die as expected. Instead, she began to thrive, returned to Japan and lived there another ten years. Many years later, this healing was accepted as the third miracle attributed to Mother Duchesne. The celebration of her canonization took place in Rome on July 3, 1988.

Shrine of Saint Philippine Duchesne, 1952

15

CONCLUSION

MOST GROUPS OF EUROPEAN MISSIONARIES
who came to America formed independent congregations in
the spirit of the life and mission they had known in Europe,
but with autonomous governance because of the long delays in
communication across the sea. Perhaps because of Madeleine
Sophie's special gift for forming loyal relationships, Philippine
refused to create an autonomous American congregation, even
when Bishop Dubourg would have liked her to, given the frus-
trations of delays as long as six months to receive a response
from France. Because of Philippine's insistence on union, the
Society of the Sacred Heart is today, more than two hundred
years later, an international congregation in forty countries with
a single united governance that has never been broken. Because
of Philippine, whose vision traveled to the horizon of the possible when the Society was otherwise focused on France, new
horizons continue to call.

Philippine's life was one of courage, vision, and generosity. With
open heart, she faced and overcame incredible obstacles in order
to bring the love of Christ to those who did not know it. Two
particular characteristics should make her beloved by those who

struggle in the same way. First, though she wanted to accomplish her life's work in younger days, obstacles of all kinds prevented her from following the call of God until she was well into middle age. Those who struggle to follow God's call for them and are prevented through many years will find in her a companion and friend. Second, though her zeal and love could overcome great difficulties, she was never able to learn the language that, after her own, would have been the most helpful for her mission. In our multicultural world, those who find their effectiveness hindered by lack of ability in languages should know that she shared their frustration and can be present as encourager and friend.

The life of Philippine Duchesne continues to inspire those with a thirst for mission and a love of the poor. Among them is Pope Francis, who has a special devotion to her. With Saints Louis and Vincent de Paul, she is co-patron of the Archdiocese of Saint Louis. The readings of the Mass for her feast on November 18 capture some of the qualities that so characterized her. Isaiah 52:7-10 begins with the allusion that Philippine herself used at her first encounter with Sophie on her mountain of Sainte Marie in 1804: "How beautiful upon the mountains are the feet of those who announce peace." The passage ends with the promise that all nations will see the salvation of God—exactly the vision that inspired Philippine to want to go out into the whole world to preach the good news. The Gospel (John 12:20-26) speaks of the personal consequences: the grain of wheat must fall to the ground and die in order to produce life, just as her sacrifice, despite feelings of failure, bore the fruit of a great harvest.

Many commentators have developed their characterization of Philippine by a play on the meaning of her family name, "of the oak." Few are aware that Philippine herself did the same thing. On June 29, 1821, only three years after her arrival in America, she wrote a letter to her dear cousin and best friend, Josephine Perier, Madame de Savoye-Rollin. Although she was only in her early fifties at the time, Philippine expressed the hope that she would die before Josephine, but added: "if God disposes otherwise, may he destine me to be an old oak that lives among the storms that destroy younger and healthier plants."

We remember the oak and we celebrate her strength.

1769 Birth of Rose Philippine Duchesne in Grenoble, France

1788 Her entry into the Visitation Convent in Grenoble, disbanded in 1792 by the Revolution

1804 Her entry into the Society of the Sacred Heart after the Revolution

1815 Election as secretary general and move to Paris

1818 Voyage from Bordeaux, France, to New Orleans with four companions and opening of the first school in Saint Charles, west of the Missouri River, on September 14

1819 Move of the community and school to Florissant on the east side of the Missouri River

1821 Foundation of the second school at Grand Coteau, Louisiana

1825 Foundation of the third school at Saint Michael, Louisiana

1827 Foundation of the fourth school, the City House, in south Saint Louis

1840 Philippine's relief from the office of superior

1841 Foundation of the mission to the Potawatomi in Sugar Creek, Kansas

1842 Return of Philippine from Sugar Creek to Saint Charles

1852 Death of Philippine in Saint Charles on November 18

1940 Beatification of Philippine on May 12

1988 Canonization of Saint Philippine Duchesne on July 3

Made in the USA
Lexington, KY
09 April 2018